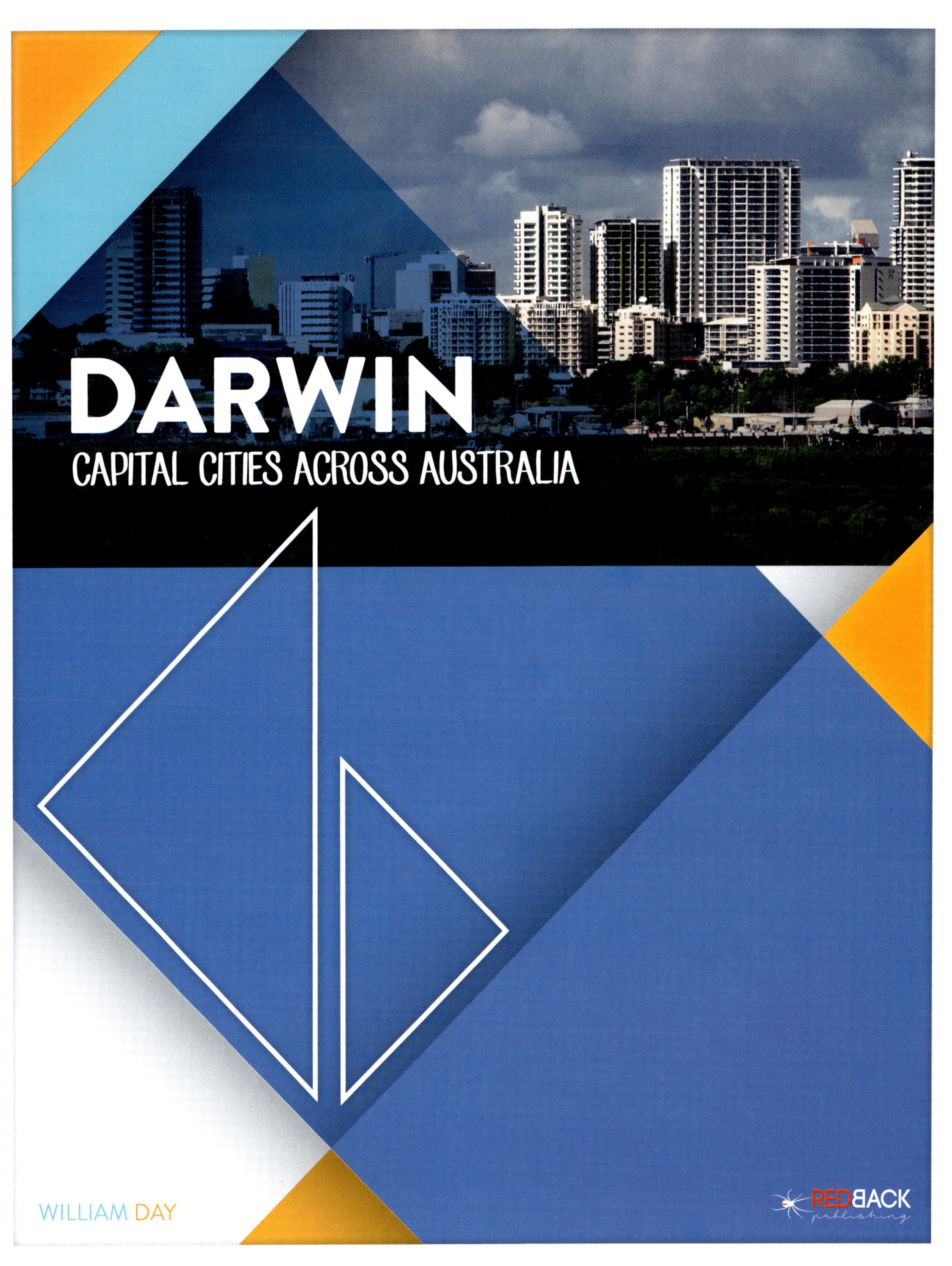

DARWIN
CAPITAL CITIES ACROSS AUSTRALIA
WILLIAM DAY
REDBACK
publishing

Redback Publishing
PO Box 357 Frenchs Forest NSW 2086
Australia

www.redbackpublishing.com.au
orders@redbackpublishing.com.au

978-1-925860-49-8

Author: William Day
Editor: Marianne Lindsell
Designer: Redback Publishing

Original illustrations © Redback Publishing 2018
Originated by Redback Publishing

Printed and bound in China by Leo Paper

Acknowledgements
Abbreviations: l—left, r—right, b—bottom, t—top, c—centre, m—middle

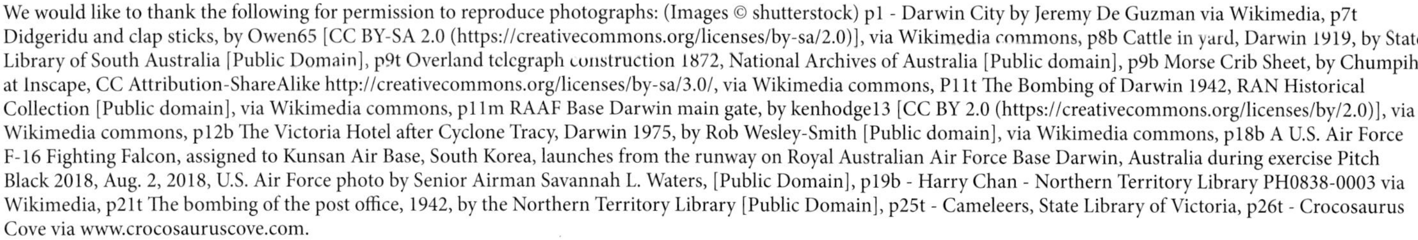

We would like to thank the following for permission to reproduce photographs: (Images © shutterstock) p1 - Darwin City by Jeremy De Guzman via Wikimedia, p7t Didgeridu and clap sticks, by Owen65 [CC BY-SA 2.0 (https://creativecommons.org/licenses/by-sa/2.0)], via Wikimedia commons, p8b Cattle in yard, Darwin 1919, by State Library of South Australia [Public Domain], p9t Overland telegraph construction 1872, National Archives of Australia [Public domain], p9b Morse Crib Sheet, by Chumpih at Inscape, CC Attribution-ShareAlike http://creativecommons.org/licenses/by-sa/3.0/, via Wikimedia commons, P11t The Bombing of Darwin 1942, RAN Historical Collection [Public domain], via Wikimedia commons, p11m RAAF Base Darwin main gate, by kenhodge13 [CC BY 2.0 (https://creativecommons.org/licenses/by/2.0)], via Wikimedia commons, p12b The Victoria Hotel after Cyclone Tracy, Darwin 1975, by Rob Wesley-Smith [Public domain], via Wikimedia commons, p18b A U.S. Air Force F-16 Fighting Falcon, assigned to Kunsan Air Base, South Korea, launches from the runway on Royal Australian Air Force Base Darwin, Australia during exercise Pitch Black 2018, Aug. 2, 2018, U.S. Air Force photo by Senior Airman Savannah L. Waters, [Public Domain], p19b - Harry Chan - Northern Territory Library PH0838-0003 via Wikimedia, p21t The bombing of the post office, 1942, by the Northern Territory Library [Public Domain], p25t - Cameleers, State Library of Victoria, p26t - Crocosaurus Cove via www.crocosauruscove.com.

Every effort has been made to contact copyright holders of any material reproduced in this book. Any omissions will be rectified in subsequent printings if notice is given to the publisher.

A catalogue record for this book is available from the National Library of Australia

CONTENTS

Saltwater crocodile

Cullen Bay, Darwin

WHERE IS DARWIN?

Darwin is the capital city of the Northern Territory. The city sits on a peninsula that juts out into the Timor Sea.

Beyond the built-up parts of the city of Darwin and its suburbs, Greater Darwin has large areas of land that are used for grazing or as nature conservation regions.

When people refer to Darwin they could mean any one of five different areas

1. The city centre
2. The city centre plus its surrounding suburbs
3. The GCCSA
4. The local government area only
5. A personal idea of where they think the city is

DARWIN FACTS & FIGURES

Population of Greater Darwin in 2016 – 137,000 people

Height above sea level – from 0 metres at sea level to about 30 metres further inland

Area of Greater Darwin – 3,100 square kilometres

Climate - Darwin has a tropical climate, with both a wet season and a dry season. The wet season runs from November to April, when there is high humidity. Monsoons and cyclones occur during the wet season.

Greater Capital City Statistical Areas (GCCSA)

The Australian Bureau of Statistics (ABS) collects data based on GCCSAs for each capital city around Australia. The GCCSA is not the same as the local government area that bears the name of the city. These GCCSAs can change if the ABS believes a city has grown beyond its previous boundaries. This means that statistics for population, areas and many other things will be different depending on whether the agency compiling them is describing the GCCSA or the local government area.

Darwin Waterfront Wharf

East Point sunset, Darwin

DARWIN'S ABORIGINAL HISTORY

The Larrakia Aboriginal people are the Traditional Custodians of the Darwin area. Their Nation has a long history of trading and cultural interaction with people from islands and countries to the near north of Australia.

The Larrakia are Saltwater People. Their traditional lands extend from the Cox Peninsula and nearby islands to the Adelaide River in the east, beyond the boundaries of modern Darwin.

Ancient History

Over 10,000 years ago, during the last Ice Age, sea levels around the world were lower than they are today. Part of the region between northern Australia and islands to the north was either dry land, or covered only by shallow sea. The Aboriginal people living in what is now the Darwin area could have easily travelled to islands to the north, and northerners could just as easily have come down into Australia.

Didgeridoo and clap stick players – One Mob Different Country dance troupe Nightcliff Seabreeze Festival, Darwin 2013

Lee Point Beach at low tide

DARWIN AND KAKADU

Jim Jim Waterfall, Kakadu

Kakadu National Park wetlands

Darwin is the closest large city to Kakadu and a major starting point for journeys to one of Australia's most famous national parks.

Providing services for tourists to Kakadu is an important industry in Darwin, and many visitors like to spend a day or two exploring the city before or after their trip to the magnificent Kakadu wilderness.

Businesses in Darwin offer guided tours, and also rental vehicles and campervans for people making their way to Kakadu.

DARWIN'S EARLY HISTORY

About 60,000 years ago

Ancestors of the Australian Aboriginal people reached northern Australia.

1600s

Dutch explorers, including Willem Janszoon and Abel Tasman, sailed through the waters north of Darwin.

1839

Captain Wickham sailed the waters of Port Darwin aboard the Beagle.

1869

After several failed attempts at settlement, Britain finally established the town of Palmerston, later to become the city of Darwin. George Goyder came from South Australia with the purpose of locating pasture that was suitable for livestock.

1871

The undersea telegraph cable link that connected Darwin with London came ashore at Palmerston. This made the city an important location for international communication.

1911

Palmerston was renamed Darwin, after Charles Darwin, the famous naturalist.

Palmerston

The British had been trying to establish a permanent settlement on Australia's northern coast since 1824. They did not succeed until 1869 when Palmerston was founded. It later became the town of Darwin.

There were four main reasons why the British persevered at creating a township, despite suffering a number of failures due to disease, the harsh climate and the isolation:

- Britain needed to show other countries that it had claimed all of Australia, including the inhospitable far north
- More convict settlements were needed
- The grasslands of northern Australia were perfect for pasturing cattle
- A northern port would make trade with India and China more convenient

Overland telegraph construction, Darwin 1872

Overland Telegraph Line

Because Darwin is the most northerly capital city in Australia, it has been a communications centre since the 1800s. The first telegraph line linking Australia to the rest of the world ran under the sea from Europe to Asia before coming ashore at Darwin.

The Overland Telegraph Line, completed in 1872, was Australia's most outstanding engineering project of its time. Connecting Darwin with Adelaide, and from there to Sydney and Melbourne, the telegraph allowed the delivery of messages by Morse Code around the world. Prior to this, the only exchange of information between Australia and other countries was through letters sent by ship.

A B C D
E F G H
I J K L M
Over
N O P Q
R S T U V
W X Y Z

1 •––––
2 ••–––
3 •••––
4 ••••–
5 •••••
6 –••••
7 ––•••
8 –––••
9 ––––•
0 –––––

End OK •••–•–
Over –•–
Roger •••–•
Starting –•–•–

. •–•–•–
, ––••––
? ••––••
' •––––•
! –•–•––
/ –••–•
(–•––•
) –•––•–
& •–••• Wait
: –––•••
; –•–•–•
= –•••–
+ •–•–•
- –••••–
" •–••–•
$ •••–••–
@ •––•–•
Error ••••••••

Morse Code

DARWIN AND THE SECOND WORLD WAR

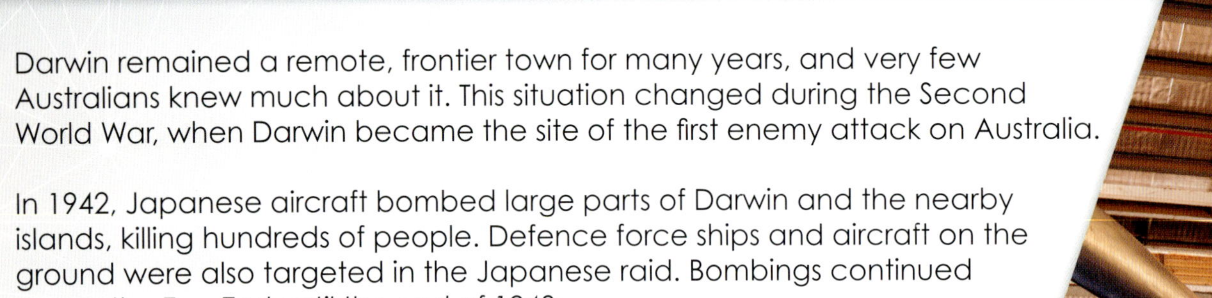

Darwin remained a remote, frontier town for many years, and very few Australians knew much about it. This situation changed during the Second World War, when Darwin became the site of the first enemy attack on Australia.

In 1942, Japanese aircraft bombed large parts of Darwin and the nearby islands, killing hundreds of people. Defence force ships and aircraft on the ground were also targeted in the Japanese raid. Bombings continued across the Top End until the end of 1943.

Civilians left Darwin before and after the attack, seeking safety in places further south.

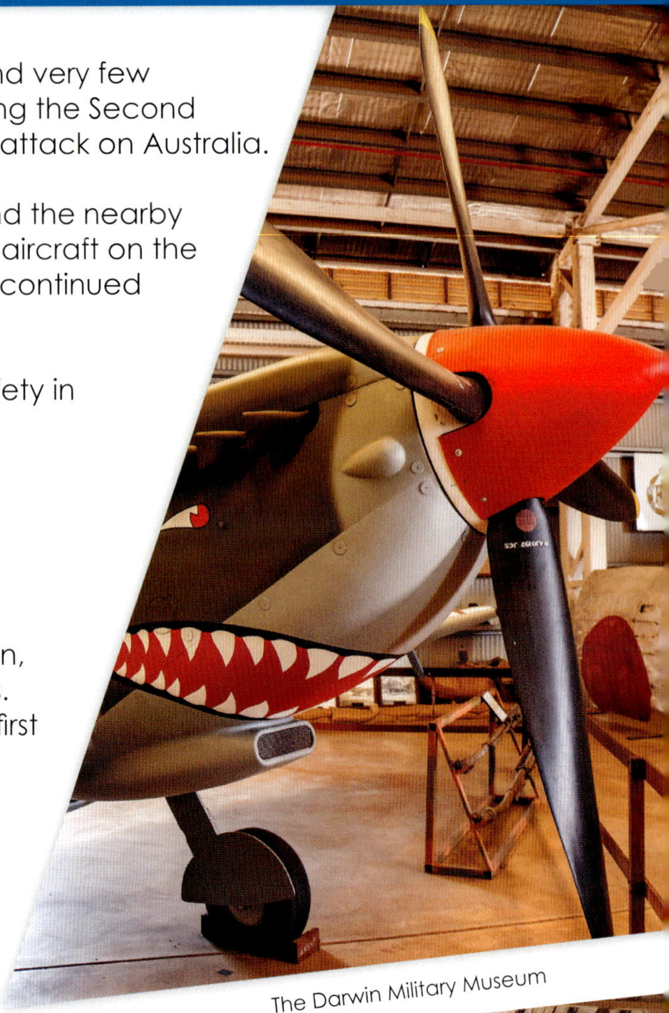

Bombing of Darwin Day

Bombing of Darwin Day is a time for solemn commemoration, when people remember those who died during the air raids. The day is held each year on 19 February, the day that the first air raid on Darwin occurred.

Darwin Military Museum

This museum is located in one of the original bunkers built as part of Darwin's defence planning during the Second World War. Displays include wartime memorabilia, artillery, photographs and vehicles.

The Darwin Military Museum

DEFENCE FORCES IN DARWIN

Darwin and the coastal region of the Northern Territory have strategic importance for Australia's defence. Members of the armed forces make up a sizeable percentage of the territory's population.

Since the First World War, and the bombing of Darwin in the Second World War, Australian governments have located defence force personnel in Darwin and used the Top End as a place for training exercises.

The defence force presence in Darwin dates back to 1824, when the British navy constructed Fort Dundas on Melville Island.

Bombing of Darwin 1942

Royal Australian Air Force Base Darwin

Bombing of Darwin 76th anniversary

RAAF Base Darwin

RAAF Base Darwin was established in 1940 and was targeted by Japanese pilots during the bombing of Darwin in 1942. Today, it plays a vital role in supporting the Royal Australian Air Force's exercises in the region. The base shares a runway with Darwin International Airport.

Barracks

Larrakeyah Barracks date from the 1930s, although some of the buildings are older. The barracks are named after the local Larrakia people, and sit on land that has sites of importance for Aboriginal history.

Robertson Barracks date from the 1990s. They are home to the US Marines when they visit to engage in joint operations with the local defence forces.

Economic Benefits

The presence of large numbers of defence force personnel in Darwin and the surrounding areas results in a large contribution to the city's economy. Defence industries make use of local businesses, as do personnel and their families, and defence housing contributes to the local construction industry.

CYCLONE TRACY

On Christmas Day, 1974, Cyclone Tracy flattened large parts of Darwin. Very high wind speeds were recorded before the cyclone destroyed the official recording instruments.

Many Australians were on holiday over the Christmas break and the people usually involved with emergency and relief services had to be called back to work. Ordinary people from all around Australia were shocked by the destruction of one of their capital cities and wanted to help. Many donated to charities to help the victims. Australia's defence forces provided much of the labour for the clean-up of Darwin after Cyclone Tracy had passed.

After the cyclone, there were few essential services left for Darwin's residents, most of whom had lost their homes. As a result, thousands of people from Darwin were evacuated to Alice Springs and other towns, just as they had been after the bombings during the Second World War.

The official evacuations were conducted according to a strict priority; pregnant women, the sick and injured were helped to leave first, while single people with no children left last. They travelled from Darwin by air or by road in buses. Some people left in their own cars. Eventually, there were only about 10,000 people left in Darwin.

Cyclone Tracy caused the largest mass movement of displaced persons in Australia's history, with about 35,000 people being rehoused in a very short time. Many of these people decided to never return to Darwin.

After Cyclone Tracy

After Cyclone Tracy, it was obvious that buildings in Darwin needed to be designed to better withstand any future cyclones of a similar ferocity.

The Victoria Hotel after Cyclone Tracy, Darwin 1975

Question: What's the difference between a displaced person and a refugee?

Answer: A displaced person has fled their home and become homeless in their own country.

A refugee has fled their home to go to a different country.

Cyclones, Hurricanes, Typhoons

Cyclone, hurricane and typhoon are all names for the same damaging weather event. The word used depends on the country where the event occurs:

- Australia has cyclones
- The USA has hurricanes
- Asia has typhoons

How Are Cyclones Measured?

There are 5 cyclone categories in Australia. Cyclone Tracy was Australia's most destructive cyclone on record, but it was only a category 4. The fact that it crossed over a city resulted in its effects being more damaging than if it had remained out over the ocean.

Did You Know?

In a cyclone, the wind circles around a central 'eye'. The centre, or eye, of a cyclone is an area of lower speed wind. Once the eye passes over an observer on the ground, the wind starts to blow in the opposite direction.

DARWIN'S BEACHES

Darwin has many beaches along the Timor Sea coastline. Unfortunately, swimming in the sea is not recommended, due to saltwater crocodiles, sharks and stinging jellyfish. Despite this, the beaches nearer to the centre of the city of Darwin are popular places with locals who know how to enjoy them safely. Other visitors to Darwin's beaches include turtles and migratory birds. These species are protected and human visitors should not disturb them in any way.

Surf Life Saving Northern Territory recommends three of Darwin's beaches for swimming when lifesavers and lifeguards are on duty. These beaches are Mindil Beach, Nightcliff Beach and Casuarina Beach.

Fannie Bay Beach

High tides can cover this beach.

Mindil Beach

The location where locals gather to watch fireworks to celebrate Territory Day each July. The markets at Mindil Beach are one of Darwin's tourist attractions.

Wave Lagoon

A swimming pool development with artificial waves for those swimmers who do not want to risk entering the sea.

Darwin City Beach

An artificial beach where swimming is relatively safe. It is located in Darwin's Wharf Precinct development.

Casuarina Beach

High tides can sometimes cover the white sand. This beach has nearby mangrove forests.

Nightcliff Beach

This beach may get its name from the landing of HMS Beagle in 1839, when explorers first scrambled up the cliffs at night using only lamplight.

CROCODILES

Crocodiles along Darwin's coast were once hunted and destroyed wherever they were found. Since they have become a protected species, the number of crocodiles has increased. They pose a threat to swimmers in the ocean and along rivers and creeks.

The Aboriginal people lived in balance with the crocodiles for many thousands of years. Colonists and settlers were unable to do this, and wanted instead to destroy as many as they could find.

Crocodiles are an important part of the wetlands biome in Darwin. People need to take great care in any location that is a crocodile habitat. Saltwater crocodiles are not confined to coastal areas and even inhabit many inland rivers.

Crocodile tourism attracts visitors to Darwin's animal parks to see crocodiles in captivity. Tourists can also take cruises to find crocodiles in the wild.

DANGER CROCODILES NO SWIMMING

Be Crocwise

The Be Crocwise Safety program encourages people to take care in areas where crocodiles live. Paddling, camping or sitting near the edge of waterways is a dangerous activity in Australia's Top End. Crocodiles wait in shallow water and may attack any animal or person on the shore.

DARWIN'S ISLANDS

Vernon Island

Channel Island

From the 1930s to the 1950s, the Channel Island Leprosarium was home to thousands of people suffering with leprosy. Leprosy is a disease that causes parts of the body to become deformed. At the time, there was no cure for this disease, and people sent to Channel Island expected to die there. The Channel Island Power Station on another part of the island provides electricity to Darwin.

Greenwood Island

A small island in the Blackmore River near Darwin.

Vernon Islands

Included in the Greater Darwin area, the Vernon Islands are located a long way north of the city of Darwin. They are mostly nature reserves and are the traditional lands of the Tiwi Islands people. The first European to sight the islands was Phillip Parker King, who named them in 1818. A lighthouse on East Vernon Island dates from the early 1900s.

DARWIN AND CLIMATE CHANGE

Governments have identified a number of possible impacts on Darwin as result of future climate change events:

- Changes in the occurrence of cyclones
- Effects on water supply
- Higher temperatures
- Effects on biodiversity of native plants and animals
- Rainfall changes
- Rising sea levels
- Coastal erosion

In response to these possibilities, governments look at making their services and their regions resilient to the effects of future climate change. They aim to do this through a range of actions:

- Conserving water supplies
- Reducing waste
- Improving air quality
- Producing energy using renewable resources
- Constructing coastal erosion barriers
- Conserving wildlife
- Reducing emissions from vehicles

DARWIN'S PEOPLE

The Australian census of 2016 revealed many interesting facts about Greater Darwin.

	Darwin	Rest of Australia
Males	52.5%	49.3%
Females	47.5%	50.7%
Aboriginal and Torres Strait Islander people	8.7%	2.8%
Median Age	33 years	

These statistics show that Darwin's people differ from the rest of Australia. There is a higher proportion of young people, more males and more Aboriginal and Torres Strait Islander people in the community.

Employment

The majority of Darwin's workers are employed by government, the defence forces and defence industries, construction businesses and in shops. The need for people with technical and trade skills in Darwin is higher than in many other parts of Australia, as shown by the statistics gathered in the last Census (2016). Greater Darwin had 17.3% of its population employed as tradespeople, while the figure for the rest of Australia was only 13.5%.

Of all the people employed in agriculture across the Northern Territory, about 60% of them work in Greater Darwin.

Royal Australian Air Force Base Darwin, during exercise Pitch Black 2018

Multicultural Darwin

Darwin is a multicultural city

- The Portuguese-Timorese community in Darwin grew in size after refugees from East Timor arrived there after 1999.
- There are also large communities of Greek-Cypriot, Filipino and Indian people in the Northern Territory, along with people from many other countries.

Top 5 foreign countries of birth for people in Greater Darwin (2016 Census)

01 Philippines
02 England
03 New Zealand
04 India
05 Greece

The Chinese in Darwin

In the 1870s, before the years of the White Australia Policy, Darwin and the whole Top End came to rely on Chinese workers to provide a labour force to help develop the settlement. The building of the Overland Telegraph Line and railway depended on Chinese labourers. The discovery of gold encouraged even more Chinese men to travel to the Top End from their homes in southern China. In the late 1800s, there were more Chinese than European men in the Top End.

The Chinese opened shops and businesses in Darwin, turning Cavenagh Street into Darwin's Chinatown. They also had market gardens all around Darwin, supplying the town with fresh fruit and vegetables.

After the end of the Second World War, people of Chinese descent began taking on roles in government. In 1966, Harry Chan became the first person with Chinese heritage to be elected as the Mayor of Darwin. He also served as president of the Northern Territory Legislative Council.

Harry Chan

DARWIN AND GOVERNMENT

The Northern Territory was a part of South Australia until 1911. It then became a Commonwealth territory until 1978 when it gained its own independent government. Territory Day is an annual event held on 1 July to celebrate this independence, and people gather to watch the fireworks on Mindil Beach and enjoy the carnival atmosphere.

Timeline of Government in the Northern Territory

01 **1825**
The colony of New South Wales expanded to include the area of the Northern Territory.

02 **1863**
South Australia took over responsibility for the Northern Territory.

03 **1888**
The whole of the Northern Territory made up just one electorate of the South Australian colonial government.

04 **1911**
An Administrator was appointed by the Commonwealth government to manage the Northern Territory.

05 **1947**
A partly-elected Legislative Council was formed.

06 **1974**
A new, fully-elected Legislative Assembly met in Darwin.

07 **1978**
The Northern Territory (Self Government) Act was passed by the Commonwealth government, giving the Northern Territory a status similar to that of the states.

08 **1998**
A referendum was held asking voters whether the Northern Territory should become a state. Their answer was that it should remain a Commonwealth territory.

Parliament of the Northern Territory

The Northern Territory has a unicameral government. It consists of the Northern Territory Legislative Assembly and the Administrator of the Northern Territory, who represents the Governor-General.

Parliament House

Parliament House sits on the site where Darwin's post office used to stand. Part of the post office wall was included in the new Parliament House building, as a reminder of the wartime bombing raid in 1942, when the post office and many of Darwin's buildings were destroyed. The new Parliament House was opened in 1994, after Cyclone Tracy destroyed the building that had been on the site since 1955.

Local Government

The first local council in the Northern Territory was the Palmerston District Council, dating from 1874. In 1957, Darwin residents elected their first municipal council.

The bombing of the post office, 1942

Parliament House

Darwin's Sister Cities

- Anchorage, USA
- Ambon, Indonesia
- Dili, Timor-Leste
- Haikou, China
- Kalymnos, Greece
- Milikapiti, Northern Territory

DARWIN'S ESSENTIAL SERVICES

Water

Black-Necked Stork (Jabiru)

Beyond Darwin, there are very few dams, and most people access groundwater through bores for their water supply. Most of Darwin's water supply comes from the Darwin River Dam. Bores at Howard Springs, 30 kilometres away from Darwin, supply the city with about 15% of its water.

Although Darwin has heavy rainfall during the monsoon season, there is also a long dry season when no rain may fall. During this time, Darwin's residents need to conserve water. As Darwin's population increases, the supply of water to the city may need to be increased through the building of more dams or of a desalination plant.

Darwin River Dam

The Darwin River Dam provides 85% of the drinking water for Darwin. Downstream, past the dam, the Darwin River joins the Blackmore River which then flows into the Timor Sea at Darwin.

The dam on the Darwin River was built in 1972 to supply Darwin's growing population with drinking water. The monsoon rains fill the dam each year, but the long dry season often results in water levels becoming low. When the dam is full, water may flow over the top and result in raised river levels downstream.

The importance of the Darwin River Dam means that access to its catchment area is restricted. This ensures the quality of the water is not affected by any human activity nearby.

What is a desalination plant?

Desalination means taking the salt out of seawater to make it suitable for people to drink and for use on gardens or in agriculture. Drinking saltwater makes people sick. Using seawater to water plants will kill them.

Darwin River Dam wall and pump

Darwin's Power Sources

Natural Gas

Natural gas was first used in the Northern Territory in 1986, when gas from central Australia was piped into Darwin to generate electricity. Natural gas is mined throughout the Northern Territory, both onshore and from offshore drilling platforms. Pipelines connect mines with power stations and with a Liquefied Natural Gas (LNG) plant near Darwin.

Electricity

In 1912, the first electricity supply to Darwin provided its residents with the luxury of ice, produced in a local factory. For many years, electricity was only available for a few hours each day, so people had to plan their use of power within those times.

Most of Darwin's electricity now comes from the Channel Island Power Station, which is fuelled by natural gas. The plant was built to withstand cyclones in the area, so that Darwin would not be subject to constant blackouts whenever extreme weather conditions occurred.

DARWIN'S TRANSPORT

Stuart Highway

The Stuart Highway is the main road route from north to south, down the Australian continent. It begins in Darwin and ends at Port Augusta on the South Australian coast.

Airports

Darwin's first airport was built in 1919. During the Second World War, the airport attracted Japanese bombing raids. Today, RAAF Base Darwin shares the runways with Darwin's International Airport traffic.

Darwin Royal Australian Air Force Base

Port Darwin

Port Darwin

With no roads or railways linking Darwin with the rest of Australia, early residents of the Top End relied on ships to transport goods and travellers.

Port Darwin is now a shipping port with facilities for container ships, cruise ships and bulk ore carriers. The Adelaide to Darwin railway line ends at Port Darwin, where there are facilities for loading bulk shipments for export.

Port Darwin is one of the busiest livestock ports in the world. About half of the live cattle exported by Australia pass through this port, with the main destinations being Indonesia and Southeast Asia.

Afghan cameleers

Railway

A railway linking Adelaide with Alice Springs was completed in 1929, but it was not until 2003 that the tracks were finally extended northward to Darwin. The passenger train linking Darwin with Adelaide is called The Ghan, after the Afghan cameleers who helped to build the railway line. A trip on The Ghan is one of the world's great train journeys. There is no commuter railway service in Darwin.

An old railway line linking Darwin to Katherine closed in the 1980s after being damaged by floods.

Buses

Commuters and school children use bus services to travel around Darwin.

Bicycles

Darwin provides many kilometres of bike paths and encourages its residents to use them when possible.

Ferries

Ferries carry passengers from Darwin to the Tiwi Islands and to Mandorah.

PLACES TO SEE IN DARWIN

- Chung Wah Temple and Museum
- Crocosaurus Cove
- George Brown Darwin Botanic Gardens
- Darwin Military Museum
- Darwin Skywalk Lookout
- Darwin Waterfront
- East Point Military Precinct
- Fort Hill Wharf

Parliament House

Royal Flying Doctor Service

- Government House
- Mindil Beach and Markets
- Museum and Art Gallery of the Northern Territory
- Palmerston Town
- Parliament House
- Royal Flying Doctor Service Darwin Tourist Facility
- St Mary's Cathedral
- Stokes Hill Wharf

Stokes Hill Wharf

BUSINESS AND INDUSTRY IN DARWIN

Mangoes

The cultivation of mangoes is one of Darwin's most high value agricultural industries, second only to meat production.

Live Cattle Exports

Port Darwin is one of Australia's main points of export for live cattle to Southeast Asia.

Defence Industry

The defence forces have a long history of involvement in the Northern Territory's Top End. Australian combined operations with overseas forces often result in Darwin hosting personnel from the armed forces of other countries.

The defence industry contributes to the Northern Territory economy by providing employment and making use of local businesses. The real estate industry in Darwin is boosted by the need for defence force housing. Darwin's Defence Support Hub, located near the Robertson Barracks, is an industrial park for businesses that supply and support the Australian Department of Defence.

Commercial Fishing

The commercial fishing industry in Greater Darwin depends on both wild-catches and aquaculture. Wild barramundi are a popular catch, as are crabs and prawns. Trepang (sea cucumber) is a delicacy, harvested by hand in strictly controlled numbers. Macassan fishermen have been visiting Australia's north for hundreds of years to collect trepang.

Australian beef cattle in Darwin ready for export to Asia

TOURISM

Tourism is a major source of income for the people of Darwin. Tourism provides employment for locals in the tourism service industries, such as restaurants and hotels.

Recreational Fishing

Located on a peninsula, Darwin is an excellent fishing base, for both recreational and commercial fishing activities.

Ecotourism

The waterways, wetlands and bushland of Australia's north are magnets for tourists, and Darwin is often their first point of call when they visit the region. The natural, unspoiled beauty of the region is an important factor for tourists, and ecotourism plays a vital role in preserving the resources for the future.

What is Ecotourism?

Ecotourism refers to tourism that does not damage the environment.

Sailing yacht at sunset, on the approach to Darwin

White Egret

EAST POINT RESERVE

Mangrove boardwalk, East Point Reserve, Darwin

This large parkland near the centre of the city of Darwin covers 200 hectares. Visitors can enjoy the nature walking trails, water sports at Lake Alexander, or visit the historic military areas. East Point Reserve contains remnants of the monsoon rainforests that used to cover large parts of the region.

The reserve provides a variety of habitats for wildlife. To ensure the biodiversity of the reserve is maintained, destructive animals such as dogs, cats and cane toads are controlled.

Mangroves, East Point Reserve, Darwin

The City of Darwin has identified a number of factors that pose threats to the biodiversity of the city's native plants and animals:

- Animal pests such as cats, dogs and cane toads kill native wildlife
- Weeds colonise native bushland
- Climate change challenges plants and animals that have adapted over thousands of years to climate conditions that suit their way of living
- Urbanisation results in the clearing of bushland and mangrove forests

GLOSSARY

aquaculture production of fish and other seafood from farms
artillery large guns and cannons
biodiversity range of plants and animals in an area
biome community of plants and animals with common characteristics suited to the environment they exist in
desalination the removal of salt from seawater
ecotourism tourism that does not damage the environment
ferocity extreme violence
hinder stop something happening
infrastructure buildings and structures needed for a society to function
Macassans old name for sailors from Indonesia and similar regions
memorabilia items that remind us of the past
peninsula landscape feature that has water on three sides and a narrow connection to the mainland
proportion size of something compared to the whole
Top End Australia's most northerly regions

Darwin Waterfront
Nightcliff sunrise

INDEX

Darwin

Litchfield National Park, termite mound